Confessions of a Serial Salesman

Confessions of a Serial Salesman

27 Rules for Influencers and Leaders that will change your
Life and Business

Steve Nudelberg

Foreward by Marc Nudelberg

Published by:

701 S Olive Ave
West Palm Beach, FL 33401

On the Ball hardcover edition June 2017

Designed by On the Ball – Michelle Esposito, Aziel Shea, David Miner

For information about special discounts for bulk purchases,
please contact On the Ball at info@ontheballmarketing.com.

Manufactured in the United States of America

Library of Congress Control Number: 2017909518

ISBN – 13:   9781981455201
ISBN – 10:   1981455205

Definitions of grow: 1. to spring up and develop to maturity: 2. to be able to develop in some place or situation: 3. to develop from a parent source: 4. to have increasing influence: 5. to promote the development of.

*To my grandfather, Sid, and my father, Stan,
who are the reason I am who I am.*

About the Author

Steve Nudelberg is an author, expert sales trainer and consultant, keynote speaker, and serial entrepreneur. Steve founded On the Ball – a company that invests time and talent in emerging businesses and corporate teams to help them grow.

Steve is often hailed as an energetic powerhouse who infuses adrenaline into a room! His core philosophy is to ignite individuals and teams by enhancing their awareness about small, yet, powerful changes they can make to instantly sharpen individual performance. Steve's 27 core leadership Rules of Engagement, within this book, have been developed over decades of corporate and entrepreneurial leadership endeavors.

As proven by great teams throughout history, greatness is achieved through developing a process or a roadmap for success, something that allows for you to deal with the many obstacles and roadblocks that everyone endures.

Steve has a long history of sales success, mentoring, and leadership. After building and leading a winning, national, sales team for ABC Cellular, Steve found himself at a crossroads. In between jobs, he started receiving requests to match companies and personalities to sponsorship opportunities, primarily in the sports arena. This gave birth to the idea of founding his own sales and marketing company that offered sales strategy, messaging, brand identity, sales and leadership training, and Arrangemenship™ (business development) as well as other services. Today, the company focuses on injecting high octane ideas and relationship capital into businesses to help teams transform and accelerate.

Companies that On the Ball has partnerships with include: Boatsetter.com, Realconnex.com, GrapeStars, Ronn Motors, and General American Capital Partners. On the Ball's list of clients include: Toshiba Business Solutions, BankUnited, The Miami Marlins, Steiner Sports, OnFire Books, Enterprise Holdings, Transworld Business Advisors, and Advaion.

Steve's specialty, within organizations, centers on creating sales processes, sales acceleration and development, the art of Building Relationships, and storytelling to make conversations engaging. Steve lives in Florida and travels the world, often on adventures and sporting events with his special lady, Michelle Esposito. This is his first book.

Forward

History leaves clues and success is never a mistake. How did I learn this? Steve Nudelberg is my dad and I am a student of his Rules and Systems. I grew up around them. Through the years of watching him develop these rules, I have learned that there are undeniable truths about successful people. As a football coach, I recently shared these truths with my team. These different truths are in the areas of: Sacrifice, Work Ethic, and Learning.

Successful people are students, teachers, and motivators who have a passion for what they do. In general, humans are creatures of habit. History repeats itself so, in order to change the future, we must study and understand the past. It's important to study the impact and benefits of routines (both good and bad) if we want to make an impact.

Why is change hard? It makes us uncomfortable. Change is often different, feels foreign, and creates fear because, when we change, we are shifting from what we know to what we don't know and we don't have the answers. We cannot pull from our own understanding the knowledge or results we expect. We may not see the results we want. There must be trust and faith and persistence. Change forces us to work harder. It does not allow you to rely on previously stored knowledge.

We must seek new answers. In order to do that properly, we have to think critically. Look at things from multiple perspectives. Adapt in order to make progress. It requires consistency.

What is change to you? We can say that we are changing and do it once. But for there to be actual change and/or growth, it requires repeated actions over a significant amount of time. "If your actions inspire others to dream more, learn more, do more, and become more, you are a leader."– **John Quincy Adams, 6th POTUS**

Seek new information. As you travel on your life journey, continually challenge yourself with new books, ideas, and knowledge. Ask yourself why you are doing the things you do and if it still makes sense to you and the people you are leading. If it does not, let it go. Invite questions and other viewpoints (Think about them) and challenge yourself to think critically. When you make a mistake, don't forget to keep moving forward. No one is perfect. We will all be wrong from time to time and we will all feel bad about something. Just, get up. Then ask why. Then try again!

Marc Nudelberg

Special Teams & Recruiting Coordinator

Lafayette College

"It's a privilege, not a right"

Introduction

Selling is about relationships.

And guess what? You're the difference maker. You're the one who makes the difference between success and failure and, ultimately, whether you will move the buyer to act. Of course, there's always that unexpected deal that falls through and, without a doubt, there are things outside of the realm of your control. We will talk about a few examples of that later in the book. But, ultimately, the game changer in the sale is YOU.

Everything hinges on relationships. How well have you worked to show your prospect that you care? Have you gone out of your way to serve them, meet with them, or communicate that you're not just after their money but that you truly care about who they are and what they do?

There's a simple rule in sales. That rule is that if they don't like you, they're not buying from you.

It doesn't matter what you sell. Whether you sell vacuum cleaners, cars, or million-dollar business deals, if you're genuinely into people and you're authentically focused on relationships, you're going to excel. If you are a people person, you will be a better salesperson than someone who is not and you'll experience accelerated success because your focus is on people versus numbers and clients and prospects will be drawn to you.

I'm a student of life. I'm just a regular guy who is observant and studies everything. I learn from conversations, movies, radio, business deals, and everyday relationships. If you're not learning, you're missing out!

One of my favorite quotes is from the movie The Godfather. "Tom, don't let anybody kid you. It's all personal, every bit of business. Every piece of shit every man has to eat every day of his life is personal. They call it business. OK. But it's personal as hell." - Michael Corleone, The Godfather (Vito's son)

I love this quote because, like many profound lines in movies, it applies to life as well. I take these lessons to heart. In fact, just like Tom Hagen played the role of consigliere (trusted advisor) in The Godfather, I, too, have a consigliere, Sam Sami. Sam has played a significant role in helping me navigate the challenges of a growing business and he is often quoted as saying, "Opportunity needs to be seized, otherwise, it will just pass you by." For anyone who doesn't take their business personally, they are bound to fail.

Another one of my favorite lines is, "Great men are not born great, they grow great." Mario Puzzo. This is my life principle, to be a lifelong learner who grows continually.

There are a lot of business rules in the dialogue in The Godfather. "A man that doesn't spend time with his family isn't a real man." Marlan Brando. Family comes first. It is something I learned early on. Everything after that is just business. Business is important, but family is more important.

How do men and women grow great? A tree doesn't just sprout up instantly in a day. It grows through dirt, and harsh weather, and drought, and sunshine, and rain. The tree keeps blooming. It grows through rain and survives winter, and sleet, and frost, and adverse conditions. It loses all its leaves and you think it's dried up and withered away because the branches look desolate but then spring comes and, boom!, the branches sprout greenery again.

Adversity creates growth. In fact, I'd go so far as to say that the most amazing leaders I've ever met have dealt with and tackled a lot of adversity in their lives. How can you overcome obstacles if you haven't had practice? A good sales person is good at blocking and tackling and, also, understands how to create opportunity. It's not about the close. It's about creating a lot of opportunity, in the first place, because sales is a numbers game.

How good are you at managing adversity? Sales people are experts at overcoming rejection and adversity and closed doors if they've been in it long enough. You cannot let those things deter you. Keep on building those connections. Power is about being a super connector and authentically building a network of influence.

At On the Ball, we guide sales people, leaders, and teams on how to develop authentic relationships (among other things). But this is a process that didn't just happen overnight. It evolved over decades of hands-on experience working with people resulting in several clients over the years saying, "Hey Steve, you're really on the ball." It evolved after countless meetings, after many years of "fifty cups of coffee," (a principle I speak on inside organizations across the world), and thousands of face-to-face meetings.

Too often in sales, teams of excellent sales people have been conditioned to believe that it's the "art of the close" that matters, as if some magical occurrence is going to happen at that point to close the deal. But I don't believe it's the art of the close at all. In fact, there's no mystical art about it. Selling is about connecting with humans. It's about investing in the relationship. It's as simple as that.

After years of selling and training others, I can say, unequivocally, that it's not the close. The close, in fact, happens earlier than you think. It happens each, and every, time someone interacts with you. For this reason, your personal brand matters.

I am often approached by total strangers in a bar or restaurant with the comment, "Love your blazer, or cool shoes, or you always look so dapper." In business, you have less than 3 seconds to make a first impression. What you wear and how you wear it matters.

In fact, the other day while checking in to an event where I was the keynote speaker, one of the ladies at registration said, "You are by far the best dressed man I have seen all day." Not bad, especially knowing there were thousands of other attendees. None of this is by accident.

People do judge the book by its cover (i.e. see the cover of this book). I credit my significant other, Michelle Esposito, as it has been her guidance and keen sense of fashion and design that has helped me develop my own personal brand. She has taken me beyond my comfort zone and has taught me that what works for me would not necessarily work for someone else.

It's all about confidence in the way you package yourself. Finding that sweet spot between getting out of your comfort zone and developing a unique and memorable identity is where the magic happens. You need to always be aware of your brand image and what you need to do to make sure that it is as good as it can be. One of our NY rainmakers, Nkrumah Pierre, rocks the bowtie. He owns it and he is unforgettable.

So, what impression do you leave on prospects, colleagues and clients? Ultimately, it is how you make them feel. Now, more than ever, we have access to everyone on social media. In an instant, I can peek into your life, see who you like, what foods you like to eat, what bars you hang out in, and what kind of people you spend time with. In an instant, someone can google you and make a split-second judgement about whether they like you or not – just based on your posts, your messaging, and your pictures.

When I train sales people, I train them about their own personal brand and how to develop it, but I also educate them about the importance of the sales funnel. If nothing goes in, nothing comes out. Sales is about touching as many people as possible, even if it's simply a phone call or a voicemail or a text at the end of a day. How intentional are you about connecting with others?

I've got 5,000 connections on LinkedIn because I believe strongly in this principle. It took time, but I reached out and cultivated a network through a series of repeatable steps. Great sales people are always thinking about who they can connect with and how.

If you're the leader of an organization, but you admittedly don't like sales, I hope this book can reframe your thinking. We are all selling something. This book is about making you realize that everything is about how you sell it.

Every organization needs leaders who can sell and understand the selling process. Selling is a function of communication and influence. Those two things drive any relationship, because we need to be excellent communicators to get people to see our point of view! It's that way in a marriage, a friendship, a board position, or a company.

The function of selling impacts how well we interact with others, both internally and externally. Being a good sales person isn't just about making your goals, in fact, it has very little to do with it.

No matter what industry you're in and what role you perform - we are all sales people. Everyone is selling something, presenting every day, and forging relationships. If you're in the role of a paid sales person, however, you've got to be better than ever at developing and strengthening relationships. When I'm talking to a group of sales people, I often ask the question, "What's the difference between a really good business relationship and a good relationship?" The answer is, there's no difference at all.

I have been friends with Michael Ralby for over 30 years. We were introduced by an old girlfriend to discuss a business opportunity and we have been friends ever since. We have shared in some incredible life experiences, both good and bad, and, yet, we continue to do business and refer each other to this very day. He once shared something with me over a few drinks that has allowed me to focus on what really matters in life "What happens if you spend your whole life climbing the corporate ladder just to realize it was leaning against the wrong wall?"

It's the relationships that matter and last forever. But humans tend to separate the two. When I can inspire people to think differently, they begin to see that it all centers on relationships. Winning centers on how well connected you are, how well you communicate, and how you're received. Are you influencing others? Build relationships.

Somewhere in the business process your company's service, support, product, performance, or technology will be tested. Nothing is perfect all the time and, when that time comes, you're continued business will be dependent on the relationships you have formed with and within your buyers.

The trust and communication you've developed in the relationship is what will make the difference. Integrate just one of these 27 rules into your life and business for just thirty days and I guarantee you'll see immediate results in your life. At the end of the day, selling is a choice and the game changer is YOU!

THE RULES
27 Rules of Engagement
for Influencers and Leaders

RULE
#1
Wake Up Early

The old adage, *the early bird gets the worm,* is for a reason. It refers to the person who gets up and slays the day before anyone else does. The sales person who works while everyone is asleep and the human who gets more done before everyone else opens their eyes!

I get up early every morning and it's turned into a routine. It allows me to get a head start on my day and I get more done in these early morning hours than most people. Most people don't wake up early—but successful ones do! It's all about routine and preparation. Remember, preparation is key. How do you prepare for your day? One thing I can count on, I may not be the best looking or the smartest, but I am always first.

I pay attention to life because success leaves clues. The very first clue I got from watching successful entrepreneurs is that they get up early. Early is relative to you personally, meaning, discover what works for you. You may work at 3am or you may work at 7am, but the time is not important. It is all about you and what works for you. Having this time for yourself is important. I have heard the same thing from several well-known and successful people. The Rock, Robin Sharma, Richard Branson, and many successful CEO's have all expressed the significant impact that getting up early has had on their personal success. Those morning hours are important to battling obstacles in your life. I once read that, in the morning hours, you are battling fear hormones. Your body uses fear hormones (cortisol) to wake you up. It is also the hormone that our body uses to keep us safe and activates our fight or flight response, as well. Why not battle them first thing? Tackle those fears, overcome them, and set up your day for success. The early morning hours help set up the success ratio of your day.

In sales, anyone who has ever delivered a critical presentation has felt nervous or were caught off guard by questions from clients following the presentation. It is not important to know every single answer, but it is important to be prepared. That preparation can help you because when you know who you are, what you are selling, and your target audience, you are far more prepared than most anyone else. Getting up early gives you the advantage. I encourage you to do it and get your day started right.

I wake up at the same time every morning whether I have to or not. I have trained myself to wake up between 3-4am and I haven't used an alarm clock in twenty years. Even if my family is still asleep or it's a holiday, I still wake up because it's a routine that I've developed which helps me get my day started. It's more about the discipline of waking up early than anything else.

A routine is what you do all the time. When you create a routine, you take control of your life. Even creating small routines for yourself can help you set boundaries and goals. Self-discipline is created by you and it's good for you. Someone once asked me the difference between routine and discipline and I had a lot to share. If your routine is going home at night and having a beer and a bag of potato chips, that is not discipline. Discipline is when you commit to doing the things you know you need to do, whether you want to or not. Discipline is a vital part of how people become successful.

Here is my first challenge for you: Take a close look at your routines, write them down, and understand what you're doing. Do more of what's working and less of what's not.

"Early to bed and early to rise, makes a man healthy, wealthy, and wise."

~Benjamin Franklin

Action Plan

_____

_____

_____

_____

_____

_____

_____

_____

_____

_____

_____

_____

_____

_____

_____

_____

_____

RULE
#2
Make Your Bed

One rule that is important to me is making my bed every day. Again, this one rule is about developing a healthy habit. It's all about being disciplined and having a routine.

Navy Seals have their beds inspected every day. They learn early on that if their bed is not made, and made just right, they are in BIG trouble. Navy Seals are uniquely trained for war-fare. They're trained killers, warriors, and military strategists—the elite of the elite—yet, they have their bed inspected every day. Part of their routine for success is to make their bed every day. It's about accomplishment—however simple! I can't get dressed when my bed is not made because it's a small accomplishment and a routine I created for myself.

The Admiral of the Navy Seals, William H. McRaven, gave a speech at the University of Texas in 2014. In that speech, he emphasized the need to train yourself to do small things well. If you do, you can do big things well. "Don't sweat the small stuff" is a nice slogan, but it isn't accurate. Successful people, and teams, are built by creating systems and processes that ensure the small stuff gets done and gets done right.

I have taken all the things I have learned and put them into a system. I teach people how to create routines and these routines increase their probability of success. The opposite is also true. If you haven't created routines for yourself, you will increase the probability that you will not be successful.

Pat Riley is one of the greatest NBA coaches of all time. I met him several years ago and I was able to do some business with him. During the process of developing our relationship, I became mesmerized by his attention to details. Pat looks at his travel schedule and then has his own sheets and towels sent in advance to the hotels where he is scheduled to stay. This attention to detail is his way of dealing with the probability of having uncomfortable towels and bed sheets. By providing his own towels and sheets, he ensures for himself, and his team, consistent comfort and a good night's sleep. Controlling these seemingly small variables, Pat increases the chances of his team having a great game. *"The only thing in life you can count on is change so you better learn to embrace it." Pat Riley*

I strive to learn from others and when I hear about someone like Pat, who is disciplined and organized, I can take tips from their life and apply them to my own. I think discipline and organization brings clarity. It frees you up to do more important things. You have to be your own boss and tell yourself how to start each day. This is the essence of self-discipline.

"If you take care of the small things, the big things take care of themselves. You can gain more control over your life by paying closer attention to the little things."

~ Emily Dickinson, 1830 – 1886

Action Plan

_____

_____

_____

_____

_____

_____

_____

_____

_____

_____

_____

_____

_____

_____

_____

_____

_____

_____

RULE
#3
In the Zone

There is a tremendous amount of negativity in the world. With all the information being thrown your way, it can be easy to become distracted and start believing that you're never going to reach your goals.

I love to ask people, from time to time, if they have ever heard of being "In the zone". Invariably they ask, "What is in the zone?" The zone is when everything goes exactly as you planned. You feel as if things flow smoothly and everything happens as you intend for it to happen. It takes practice to reach this level of tranquility. For the average person, hitting all the green lights, walking into a line-free Starbucks, or arriving at the office and receiving that amazing call you have been waiting for would be examples of being "in the zone". Things like that make you feel euphoric!

So, where did this term come from? It was coined by Michael Jordan

At the 1992 NBA finals, the Chicago Bulls were playing the Portland Trailblazers. If you could match the feeling of being in the zone with a number system, say a scale of one to a ten, what would your self-assessment be? Maybe you strive to be a ten most of the time, but not all the time. Michael Jordan believed that in everyday life, it was physically impossible to be a 10 all the time. He believed you would burn out. You have to be able to assess yourself if you want to be the best of the best. If you woke up in the morning and gave yourself an assessment, what would your number be? Would you wake up in the morning and be a five or do you wake up incredibly joyful and on fire for life? I have a friend who has a note on her bathroom mirror that says, "Be an eleven not a ten." She admits that she began using that mantra after noticing she was becoming too casual about the effort she put into her attire and taking too little time to prepare. If being a ten, or the best you can possibly be, required you to spend more time in planning and preparation, would you do it?

As my good friend Dan Lier, Best Selling Author and Motivational Speaker who I worked with early on in my career says, "Everyone has something inside of them where they want to be the best they can be and maybe they don't know how. So, learning specific tools and strategies can help get you to be better leaders, professionals, better sales people, better husbands, and wives etc.....". Some people spend their days thinking, "I didn't eat healthy today and I didn't work out" or "I didn't get that project done at work and now I'm stressed out". Whatever the situation, the difference between being good and great is figuring out what you need to do to get from a five to a ten. Maybe you can push yourself harder or raise your standards. You are the only one who can answer that question.

I am often asked why someone would need to operate at a level ten. Why not accept where they are and be comfortable? Here is my answer: Is it enough to be less than a ten with your kids and your family? Of course not. What about your job and your clients? Would it be okay for you to be less than a ten for your next prospect or your employees? Do you desire for them to see you at your very best? Being a ten is all about excellence and commitment.

I once delivered an amazing presentation to 50 bankers. During the break, one of the gentlemen came up to me and wanted to share something. He said, "A friend of mine was a ballerina and she had a lot of emotional ups and downs. But what she learned, as a professional, is that every time she had a performance, for some of the audience, it was their first time watching. That meant every night was opening night." Imagine if every performance you delivered was just like opening night.

If you operate from that mentality, where it is always opening night, then it is game time. That's what it's like to operate in the zone. If you show up feeling like a five, you know that the people in the audience deserve to see you at a ten. That changes your mindset because now the goal is to be a ten for every person, whether you feel like it or not. When the focus is on the recipient, it's about their experience and not yours. That makes it easy to want to be a ten.

With our Ballerina example, just because she has performed the same show a hundred times, she knows that there could be fifty people in the audience who have never seen a performance before and they invested their time and money to see her perform at the same level she did on HER opening night.

I like to box and my boxing trainer has taught me a lot of important skills that translate both inside and outside of the ring. Muhammad Ali was arguably one of the greatest boxers in the world and he said, "The fight is won or lost far away from witnesses, behind the lines, in the gym, and out there on the road long before I dance under those lights." His words illustrate how preparation is the key to success. In boxing, I find it amazing how long a 3-minute round can feel when you're squared off against an opponent. More so than in most sports, boxing places a premium on optimal conditioning. If you step into the ring for a sparring session without this, you probably won't be competitive. My boxing coach, Ian Curran (an ex-boxer himself), says, "The zone is a place where you stop thinking and live inside your instinct. When there is intensity and chaos but the mind is calm. Like an ocean without a ripple. This is where you have an unfair advantage over your opponent and competition. Why? Because you are a zone performer."

When I was speaking to the group of bankers who expected me to show up and deliver a level ten performance, I asked them this question, "Would it be okay if I had a bad night and then came here for my presentation and gave you a five?" Of course not! My job is to be a ten for everyone and not just for myself. That doesn't mean we can't have bad days. It just means that you can prepare yourself to give your very best in every situation. If you show up feeling like a five and your house is on fire, no one needs to know! No one needs to know what is going on in the background of your life. That isn't part of your job. Your job is to show up and be the best that you can be. Don't bring your drama with you.

The Zone is where Magic Happens. When you're in the zone, you'll know it. In the zone, you're on fire. You know it and you can't miss the mark. Common sense tells you that you cannot operate at that level every minute of every day. Some days you feel sick, other days you feel great, but if you have a plan for success, it will increase your chances of doing great. What you learn is that even when things aren't going well, you recover more quickly because of that plan and preparation. The wheels don't come off because you've trained yourself to have a system and a process.

"Limits, like fear, is often an illusion."

~Michael Jordan

Action Plan

_____

_____

_____

_____

_____

_____

_____

_____

_____

_____

_____

_____

_____

_____

_____

_____

_____

_____

RULE
#4
Exercise for Twenty Minutes Everyday

One of the keys to success is consistency. If you're not consistent, your plan will fail. It doesn't matter if your goal is to run a 5k or workout three times a week. Consistent action is the key to success in every area of life. Work out every day even if it's just a twenty-minute walk or run. If you have a habit to do this, your body and mind will perform better.

If you get up and warm up, it's possible that better things will happen. I'm not a health expert or a doctor, but I believe the experts who maintain being physically active each, and every, day leads to longevity. Physical movement isn't just about the body either. It's also about energizing the brain by increasing blood flow. In treatment for depression, one strategy that many therapists recommend is daily activities, such as exercise, to produce momentum. Experts agree that physical activity can change the way you feel, as well as the way you perceive your life and the world. We all know someone who received a new lease on life through exercise. It doesn't matter what you do as long as you do it. Walk or run twenty minutes each day.

The key is to create the habit of doing it. Of course, none of us have enough time, but it's not about time, it's about developing a routine. Every day you brush your teeth and you do it if you feel like it or not. You know you need to do it, so it isn't a question of if you want to, you do it because it is what is best for your oral health. Working out is, exactly, the same. Make it a normal part of your routine. Twenty minutes a day is all you need. This is the mentality of discipline and self-care.

So, where do you start? Write your goals and reminders on the mirror. Give yourself reminders to help you succeed. Simple phrases, like "Walk every day" or "Just do it", can have a powerful impact on your mindset. Find a quote that inspires you personally and live by it.

Humans make life much more complicated than it needs to be. Keep it simple and just add it into your daily routine. Don't think about how long it takes to workout or how much sleep you need. Don't compromise and tell yourself you'll work out on the days when you don't have that 8am meeting. Take the stairs, walk around the block, run a mile on the treadmill, and do your sit-ups before you get into the shower. Move your body every day.

One of the things I've learned about success is that you must truly want it to move towards it. You can't motivate anyone who doesn't want to be motivated. Think about what you're doing right now. What were you doing ten minutes before you started to read? You made the decision to read this book. Nobody forced you to do it. That means you've learned something new, or perhaps you have been energized or inspired to try new things or create a new pattern.

Whatever you've taken from our time together - congratulations - because today is a new day. If you feel like you've lost ground, or you want to lose a few pounds, or you just have too much on your plate, take a deep breath. You're not alone. You are the only person who can change your health.

Health is a mind, body, and spirit connection. You have to be psychologically, physically, and emotionally fit to have true health. When one area does not function, the other two can suffer. Think of how stress contributes to the aging process. Blood pressure rises, digestion stops, and cortisol levels rise. Through our stress, our lifestyle, and our diet, we are only hurting ourselves. You need to train the mind, body, and spirit for each of them to function properly.

This is the reason I took up boxing. In boxing, there are a few core essential elements. One is to always keep your toe pointed towards your opponent. This helps you learn direction. Another is to always keep a good stance, not too wide or too narrow. This helps you learn balance. I like boxing because it challenges me. It challenges my body but it also challenges my mind. Boxing reminds me that I am my biggest opponent and that it's up to me to decide between fight or flight. In one of my training sessions, I was asked to wear a harness attached to a tire with a thirty-pound weight inside. My trainer said, "The weight represents the stress in your life. How it drags on you and makes simple tasks harder." When he lifted that weight off me, I was free to kill it!

In boxing, there's a lot going on in the ring. My trainer taught me that you need to build a house around your face and body. If the hurricane is coming, you wouldn't open the window, right? You've got to keep the barrier up and you must defend. Your opponent is always looking for the opening. Boxing is a magnificent yet defensive dance. In the movie South Paw, there was a fighter who fought out of anger and his trainer said, "Your anger is taking away your capability!" Anger can fuel you, but sometimes it can derail you. Mike Tyson said, "Everyone has a plan until they get hit in the face." If you get hit in the face, in life or business, you've got to know how to react. Exercising your body keeps you mentally strong. How are the two related? It's the consistency of habit, muscle memory, and the building of strength. It's the same in life as it is in business. If you're lazy about your exercising routine you're probably also lazy in other areas of life.

I like to challenge people to see things in a different way. Most people need to be challenged for them to move out of their comfort zone. I like to remind people that no matter the situation, it is important to master the basics.

In boxing, the four basic punches are the jab, straight, uppercut, and hook. Every boxer will throw thousands and thousands of them in an attempt at mastery. Life is about mastering the basics. That's what the rules in this book are all about. There's a basic foundation to human performance and these rules are built on the things I've observed with successful people.

Think about what happens after we fall off the wagon when it comes to food and taking care of ourselves. For me, in 2016, after months of living it up, I stepped on the scale and it read 212 pounds and that was enough for me to want to make a change! I decided to try a new diet and it involved extreme discipline. Eating and drinking is a part of everyone's life but I indulged in it to the point where I found myself needing to make a change. I wanted to lose weight, get healthier, and I was ready to be extreme. For lunch, I was allowed three and a half ounces of lean protein and my calorie cap was 500 a day. Imagine that! 500 calories! But it worked.

I decided to interject something extreme into my life to get back into shape. For the diet I chose, my breakfast everyday consisted of one piece of Melba toast and a cup of coffee. The science behind the diet was that it was rooted in certain food combinations. I could have strawberries, apples, oranges, and grapefruit but no other fruits, breads, processed carbs, and limited meat. It was a strict, regimented diet. I lost a pound a day on the diet, while being extreme about my discipline.

That plan was not sustainable for a long period, but it worked to jumpstart my health and metabolism. There's nothing wrong with bold gains or goals. You can set a goal to run a full marathon but you must have a consistent exercise routine. Many marathon runners train one mile at a time and you can reach your goals in the same way.

When I first began the diet, my boxing trainer told me to run with a twenty-pound medicine ball. He told me to run a lap with it down the road and visualize what it's like to have that extra weight. Can you imagine how that feels? People who are overweight are naturally a little more sluggish than others. Your physical health impacts your mental health, and it all impacts your brand. What kind of brand do you have?

At some point, we all may struggle with fitness or body issues but it's important to be self-aware and healthy, which takes discipline. If you do wrong things, you're going to get wrong results. If you do the right things, you're going to get right results! What if you feel like you've gotten so far behind that you just can't succeed? Stay encouraged and keep believing in yourself. Keep your mind open to the possibilities that you can win even if you are down.

While watching the New England Patriots play the Atlanta Falcons in the 2017 Super Bowl, the Patriots were down 28-3. I was certain the Patriots would lose the game, but guess what? I was wrong. It was the most incredible thing I've ever seen because they never once stopped believing that they could win. And they did win. If you don't have faith in yourself or your circumstances, stop and ask yourself why. Why aren't you confident that you can do it? Why don't you have faith in your own discipline? Maybe it's because you haven't tried or set the bar high enough. Maybe you don't have a system or process in place.

God speaks in many ways and you must be open to listen. Defeat is a part of life but it doesn't mean that you'll be defeated forever. The obstacle might last a day, a week, or even a moment. I tell people that it isn't necessary to chuck tires across a highway, do cross fit, or run twelve miles. But your body is a machine and needs to be warmed up. Learn from others by watching an athlete on video or in person. Observe their habits and apply them to your life. You may not feel like working out in the morning but you can achieve the best workout from that early morning time. Before the daily grind starts, take care of your own body first.

It's in the overcoming that you win. For me, knowing that I have these rules to rely on is a comfort but also a guide that keeps me on track. Creating morning rituals can help you take care of your body and your mind. What you think, say, and do dictates your success. Everything has a series of steps.

Don't rely on your partner, your friends, or anyone else. When you take that first step out of bed and get your body warmed up, think of your health and wellness. Touch your toes, stretch to the ceiling, whatever it is you do - don't take that first step for granted. Understand your physical and mental capabilities and make a ritual of saying to yourself, "I am able to do this, so I should." Don't get caught up in analyzing the kind of exercise you're going to do, just do it. Pick something you love and do it. You don't have to be a marathon runner, a boxer, or a yoga expert. Just pick something that will get your body in shape, your blood flowing, energize you, and do it. Don't make excuses. Everyone has twenty minutes in a day.

"All truly great thoughts are conceived while walking."

~Friedrich Nietzsche, Twilight of the Idols

Action Plan

_____

_____

_____

_____

_____

_____

_____

_____

_____

_____

_____

_____

_____

_____

_____

_____

_____

_____

RULE
#5
Drink Something Green

Success leaves clues. When I set out to develop the habits of success, which I could follow regardless of what I was doing, I noticed that many of the successful people I encountered seemed to have a strange fascination with drinking things out of a blender. The more I observed successful people, the more I noticed green drinks, kale smoothies, or blended combinations of fruits and veggies they were drinking every morning.

Over the years, I've had many conversations with successful people about the way they live. One thing they all have in common is that they compress their success in fitness and food by blending their vegetables into a green drink. It might be difficult to have nine servings of vegetables a day but not if you put those vegetables into a drink.   You've got to fuel your mind and body well. "Drinking something green will change your life," says Zack Stein, President of On the Ball and the owner of Raw Republic Micro Juicery. "I learned that living a healthy lifestyle is crucial in bringing positive vibes. You will have more creativity and the ability to think is much clearer when you adopt this way of life."

When I deliver this lesson, some people don't understand it or agree. They think drinking green drinks is for tree huggers. But the truth is that everyone should be doing it, every day. Not, once, in a while, but every day.

Success leaves clues. If you want to evaluate why you're in a slump, or figure out how you can be healthier, look at what successful people do. So, what's the first step? I advise everyone to invest in a blender. My top choice is the Nutri-bullet which, at the time of this writing, is the number one selling appliance in America. In four seconds, you can mix things up and put the right fuel into your body. Many people use chia seeds and protein, while others create a mix of kale or other greens. Whatever you use, make a healthy mixture and add something green.

If you're overweight or tend to over-indulge, you can turn it around by drinking green drinks and infusing your body with nutrients. This really works! Start today by making your own at home and improvise by buying them at whole foods or other stores that carry them. Don't allow yourself to get discouraged. It doesn't matter how long you've let yourself go. Fitness and restoration begins the moment you start taking positive steps towards it. The green drink is a fast and simple way to detox and immediately begin improving your health.

There are many benefits too. Physical and emotional strength and giving your digestive system a break to name just a few. Some people love the concept of juicing so much that they go on thirty-day juice fasts and eat nothing else. Many swear by it and some people fast by giving up meats, or other foods. No one can know what's best for you except for you and your healthcare professional. But fasting has been around since biblical days and millions have talked about the benefits of it. When you give your digestive system liquids, you feel lighter and healthier.

No matter what healthy eating program you focus on, the changes will be real and instantaneous. Your body and mind will feel stronger. The correlation between physical and emotional strength is astounding. Instead of eating fried, processed foods and over indulging in alcohol or sugary desserts, you'll find better ways to fill your time and needs. Humans often resort to things they think they need to deal with stress or simply to enjoy life along the way. It takes a certain amount of wisdom to wake yourself up and realize that they're all crutches. You don't need to drink, overeat, or overindulge. When you over indulge, you know exactly what you're doing. I know what I'm doing when I eat or drink too much during a client dinner. I also know what I'm doing when I'm working out and eating clean. No one makes me do either. It's my choice and it's yours too. Today is the first day of the rest of your healthy life!

"Look deep into nature and then you will understand everything better."

~Albert Einstein

Action Plan

_____

_____

_____

_____

_____

_____

_____

_____

_____

_____

_____

_____

_____

_____

_____

_____

_____

_____

RULE
#6
Count Your Blessings
(Have Gratitude)

One of the things I've noticed about successful people is that they ooze gratitude. Even in times of struggle, they seem to have an attitude of gratitude. Unsuccessful people, on the other hand, don't. They're the ones who get caught up in the negatives on a consistent basis and always see the negative side of things.

I can honestly say that I wake up thankful each, and every, day for the things I've been given. It wasn't always that way but I have evolved over the years. Now, I take nothing for granted.

Make a conscious effort to cultivate gratitude. Whether you make a list of the things you are grateful for and post it on the bathroom mirror to remind yourself or write in a daily journal, establish the habit of reminding yourself why it's an amazing day to be alive! The incredible Zig Ziglar had a saying - "Make today worth remembering!" People who don't are consistently unhappy with their lives. Why? Maybe it is because they think tomorrow is guaranteed or perhaps they don't believe that they have what they need. If you think about it, and look around at your life, you'll see that you really do have more than enough of what you need. There is always someone who is getting by with much less.

Having gratitude is to understand what is personally good for you, in the past and present. I am grateful for so many things: my lady, my sons, my business, and my friends. So many of my friends have come through an initial business contact. Two that come to mind are my friends Bob Snyder and Byron Dennis, commonly known as my brothers from other mothers. I love these guys so much and they have been there with me through thick and thin. They have both made my life richer and I am grateful for them and others like them every day.

If you had a great childhood and great parents, check that off the list and realize that many people did not. If you have a high metabolism, no allergies, an immunity to colds, those are things to be thankful for. Not to mention a roof over your head. Nick Vujicic has no arms or legs but manages to speak all over the world for a living. He often gets paid fees that some speakers would only dream of receiving. Imagine the gratitude he has for being able to live his dream and inspire others! Zig Ziglar also said, "Gratitude is the healthiest of all human emotions. The more you express gratitude for what you have, the more likely you will have even more to express gratitude for." Gratitude is a choice and you can find it even when it seems there is nothing to be grateful about.

I'm sure you've heard the importance of having an "attitude of gratitude" -- leading entrepreneurs, bestselling authors, multi-millionaires, and celebrities all do. Focusing on the positive aspects of life help to calm anxiety and increase overall happiness and fulfillment. "You cannot be grateful and angry at the same time. You cannot be grateful and fearful at the same time." -- Tony Robbins, multimillionaire, entrepreneur, life strategist, author, and philanthropist. Robbins takes three minutes each morning to focus on feeling deeply thankful for three things starting with something simple and non-material, like the wind on his face.

The thing that gets me through my toughest moments in business and life (I call them curve balls) is gratitude. Even when I lose on a big deal or something that I expected doesn't happen, there is always something to be grateful for.

During the early years of our company as a sports marketing firm, the local hockey franchise needed to find a new naming rights sponsor. They said we're willing to give your company a 90-day shot to find a title sponsor. It would have been a multi-million dollar deal for me for ten years or so. I was with the client, ready to get the deal signed the next day, and my cell lit up. It was the CEO of the franchise. "The board voted to go with a different title naming partner," he said. "I'm sorry man." he said.

It was a punch in the stomach. I mean, a very big punch. What could have meant multi-millions of dollars went out the door in an instant. Did I do anything wrong? No. When I looked back, I saw that I wouldn't have changed a thing! For one reason or another, they simply made a different choice, and you can't choose for the buyer or seller, you can only do your best. At times, there may be other things going on in the background that you're unaware of. These things will be completely out of your control.

It was a challenging day but I rebounded. I learned that day that you have no control over the sale. There are a lot of different variables. Sell, but sometimes your sale will fall through. Great sales people have more in play than others. I did everything right in this sale. If I had to go back in time, I would've done everything the exact same way. You can think you're the greatest thing since sliced bread but, you actually have no control over the sale. How many times have you felt like you had a slam dunk but, for whatever reason, the sale fell through? I knew that despite losing the deal, I was grateful for the lesson. Sometimes you can only do your best.

Gratitude can be a tough lesson. I was forced the hard way to recognize that there is always something to be grateful for. When you see someone who is sick or suffering from something, it's easy to realize how fortunate you are. It's easy to have gratitude for what you have. Your life can change in five minutes so you'd better have gratitude for what you have in the now.

When my son was twenty, he was in an unfortunate accident that left him lying in a coma in a hospital bed for a good piece of time. If you are looking for a way to rearrange your priorities, just get a call that someone you love is sick or has died. Boom! Thankfully, my son recovered 110 percent, but that experience changed us all. Success is about process and mindset. Say to yourself, "I will be grateful for everything I have and focus on those things."

Gratitude starts there. It's a mindset. Sales people have a lot of opportunity to test their gratitude. If you're the VP of a sales team, a CEO, or any other position, you are tested with challenges and problems every day. But a sales person faces rejection on a continual basis. Sales isn't for the weak or faint of heart. If you're going to give up easily or throw in the towel, the first, second, or even the seventh time you're rejected, evaluate yourself and whether, or not, you can handle it. Sales people get rejected, kicked in the teeth, and sent away. You've got to man or woman up and keep on creating opportunity.

You've got to respond to the ones who rejected you with gratitude and figure out what you can learn from the experience. As hard as it may seem, you can have gratitude for your failures too.

"Gratitude turns what we have into enough, and more. It turns denial into acceptance, chaos into order, confusion into clarity...it makes sense of our past, brings peace for today, and creates a vision for tomorrow."

~Melody Beattie

Action Plan

_____

_____

_____

_____

_____

_____

_____

_____

_____

_____

_____

_____

_____

_____

_____

_____

_____

_____

RULE
#7
Read and Write

Readers are leaders. That's been true with most of the successful people I've met. Every one of them reads, be it books, online blogs, articles, or eBooks. They read and they grow.

It's easy to get lost in our online world today and spend hours connecting on social media without, actually, learning something new. Set a goal to read because, when you read, you will learn. When you read, you are taking in more information and, if you make time to read and journal, you will see huge changes in your life. Isn't it ironic that we would all agree that children should read but then we resist it ourselves as adults? Why wouldn't we want to read to discover the things that others have been through?

History leaves clues. When I began journaling, I discovered that it was a great way to capture what I had learned. What I learned about journaling was that I can recognize patterns. A lot of what I speak on and teach on is from seeing patterns. By keeping a journal, I could review my own patterns and observe that I am generally more motivated in January then I am in June. It helped me be more self-focused. When you see it, you can create a plan for success based on strengths or weaknesses. If you write it down and you read it, your own history can leave clues. The only way you can evaluate those clues is if you write them down and then read about your successes and your failures.

Great people who have traveled on this journey of life have written books and left all those clues behind. We've all read books written by some of the world's greatest leaders. We can learn from someone's victories, as well as their mistakes.

There is another way that writing is important. Information. If you don't write it down, how can you remember it? Sounds simplistic, but it's true. Since the beginning of time, leaders have written during meetings and for communication. Write what you hear and don't be afraid to be seen writing things down. When you write something down, it shows you care enough to record the moment.

I am always writing notes. When I go visit someone, I always take out a journal or a piece of paper and I ask people, "Do you mind if I take notes? I want to remember what you say." I learn something every day from what I write down. If you want to create your own "aha" moments, you do that by read-ing and writing.

Throughout the years, I've often gone back and read something I wrote in a journal along the way. It's amazing to see how much insight you had about life years ago, what stage you were going through, or how far you've come. When you write down where you are, what your thoughts are, and what you've learned, it can always help someone else.

My son is a college football coach and he spends a lot of time watching films. That is his reading. He's reading the defensive and offensive game plans. There is so much intake of information that it makes him smarter because he's continually learning and growing. It creates a natural instinct the next time he sees it because he's seen it already. Think of this in the way an athlete trains and creates a habit or muscle memory. The more you do something, the more natural it feels. If you're not naturally inclined to read, set a goal to stop and read a chapter each day and make notes about what you've learned. Think about the ways that reading and writing can add to your own growth plan. No matter what industry you're in you can always benefit from learning more.

"A house without books is like a room without windows."

~Heinrich Mann

Action Plan

_____

_____

_____

_____

_____

_____

_____

_____

_____

_____

_____

_____

_____

_____

_____

_____

_____

RULE
#8
You Gotta Learn to Earn

One of the traits I've found with winners is that winners win because they have an open mind. They are lifelong learners. Every winner I've met is open to learning new things.

When I spoke to a group of CEO's in Tampa Florida, they were thrilled with some of the advice I gave them. Why would a group of CEO's want to hear what I have to say? They've achieved the highest level inside of the organization because they're winners. CEO's win. But they're open to learning more about sales and life from an outsider because they are winners.

The speaking engagement in Tampa was a home run. It was a group of one hundred CEO's and they all responded very well! Winners like to learn. Don't underestimate your wisdom and knowledge.

Soon, I'll be doing a four-city tour with a bank training their teams on a variety of specific topics ranging from the Rules of Engagement to personal branding to business development. Their senior VP had called me and wanted me to focus on helping his team achieve more. It was a strong team but he wanted to help them elevate to another level and the last time I spoke to them I handed out a worksheet and at the top of the page it said "Do The Hard Things". I asked them to list the difficult things they faced in their industry each and every day. It was real and honest. It worked because it allowed them to talk about the real things they encounter versus fluff and inspiration. When you do hard things, you overcome obstacles and make the commitment to uncover them. You can't do the hard things if you're avoiding them! For most people, these things involve getting out of their comfort zone. Learning new things requires being open to learning new things and getting out of your comfort zone.

I met Tony Nugent, a retired MET Life executive, and had the opportunity to talk to him about what he did. I just asked him, "Can I pick your brain?" He had a completely open mind and was thrilled to share with me about business and life. When I meet people like this, I am always thinking, "What can I learn from them?" Why? I am constantly learning. When I was talking to Tony, I had no opportunity to sell him. It was about learning who he was. I have done that my whole career. No matter what my age is, I know that I still have so much to learn. Tony had developed a specific time grid for his team on how he recommended someone spend their time. He would ask people; "Show me your calendar." He said that he could determine a successful or unsuccessful person by the way their calendar looked.

He recommends:

60% face to face

30% preparation and training

10% admin

If you looked at your own day and week, how would you organize your schedule? Be intentional about learning and all the other things that make up your day and your business.

In the words of my favorite entrepreneur, Warren Struhl, "Teach me!" Warren is an insatiable learner. He wants to know everything there is about everything! If you learn, you may gain knowledge and tools that come in handy later. Remember, Success Leaves Clues! You may not need it now but you'll use it at some point."

"A wise man can learn more from a foolish question than a fool can learn from a wise answer."

~Bruce Lee

Action Plan

_____

_____

_____

_____

_____

_____

_____

_____

_____

_____

_____

_____

_____

_____

_____

_____

_____

_____

RULE
#9
Listen to Music

Countless studies have proven that music enhances performance. Athletes have used music for years, wearing headphones with their favorite playlist before a game to get themselves fired up, relaxed, or in the zone.

Everybody likes to listen to different genres and songs, but the consistent data is that music can motivate and inspire, and it can also create a flow state which involves an altered state of reality. Some NFL players listen to rap to get ready for their game. Others like country or pop. Other athletes have been known to have superstitions about the type of music they listen to. I love to listen to music because it easily changes my state of mind. When I speak on stage, I ask them to queue up the song "Happy" by Pharrel when I'm about to illustrate this point. No matter what kind of music you like, everyone gets joyful when they hear this song. If you don't get happy when you hear Happy there's a problem!

For years, everyone in sports has known that music has a big effect on the mind and the body. We all have a favorite song. Think about the way that song makes you feel and reproduce that feeling often during the day. Music activates the brain's reward system – the part of the brain that signals to us whether something is important, valuable, or necessary for survival. When we hear music that we enjoy, our brain releases dopamine and we experience a natural high. It's the same process that happens when we eat or exercise. Music will impact energy levels.

Have you ever worked out or run without music? There's nothing worse. And similarly, there's nothing better than when a song comes on that energizes and excites you into a peak physical state. Music influences the way you see the world and interact with others.

Researchers from the University of Groningen found that people will be more apt to recognize positive aspects of their surrounding environment when they are in a positive mood themselves. Play happy music, feel better, and you'll have a more pleasant perspective.

Start your day with it; play music in your bathroom while you're brushing your teeth. Play music on Alexa and ask her to play your favorite song or station. Download a workout playlist for the gym or that twenty-minute walk you're going to do every day. Start incorprating music into your life.

Somewhere along the way you may have found that your love for music disappeared. We discover it, first as kids. We embrace it as teens and, then in our cars when we learn to drive, we blare it in college and attend concerts. Music becomes a vital part of who we are. But, then as we develop and grow, we begin to focus more on the news, our jobs, and television at home or the Internet, and business.

Listening to music in the morning is so much better than what most people do, which is to get up and turn on the negative box or CNN (Constant Negative News). And it's unintentional. No one intentionally thinks; "Let me just turn this on so that I can get bombarded with everything that's wrong with the world and then I can go out and try to be a good person." It's impossible. How many people watch the news in the morning? Here's the story…if the world ends, you'll know it. You don't need the news to tell you.

Music will change your psychological being, which will make you better at whatever you do. If it's great for elite athletes, it can work wonders for your performance as well. Music changes your mindset. It is also a big part of visualization. Many elite athletes visualize their success before it occurs. This is a significant strategy that many people forget to do - visualize what it's like to be successful.

NFL players who have made it to the Super Bowl are dreaming about what it's like to catch that last pass and win the Super Bowl trophy for everybody. They're already dreaming it. That's what the power of visualization does. But, the vast majority of the world doesn't visualize. They don't pay attention to the clues. Don't forget - "Success leaves clues."

"One good thing about music, when it hits you, you feel no pain."

~Bob Marley

Action Plan

_____

_____

_____

_____

_____

_____

_____

_____

_____

_____

_____

_____

_____

_____

_____

_____

_____

_____

RULE
#10
Make it a Habit to Smile

Selling is about relationships with people which means that the best strategy you could deploy would be to engage and connect with people! Sounds simple, doesn't it? It actually is!

Smiling is the easiest way to transfer emotion, to set the tone for a conversation, and change a bad one. It's an instantaneous transfer of positive energy! Next time you are at a red light, look to the left and to the right. Are those people smiling? It's rare! You'll catch them texting, talking, or grimacing but you won't find them smiling. When I tell someone this for the first time, they are almost dumbfounded. Smiling takes intentionality. Remind yourself to increase your energy by smiling.

I suggest to all salespeople who work with us, to work in front of a mirror. If you're at home on the phone and you're working stand in front of a mirror and watch yourself and the emotion you transfer.

Those emotions go through the phone. Smile! People can feel it! Think about the last time you were on the phone with a customer service rep, were they smiling? What was the mood or the emotion that was part of your conversation?

Engaging with people is simple. It's the simplest thing you can do. It's a choice to make eye contact and give them your full attention. You can choose not to and you can choose to go around grumpy or focused on yourself. Or, you can make the choice to smile. I believe if you just add this one strategy to your life for thirty days that it will change your outcomes. Smiling draws people to you. In order to attract people, you've got to be joyful. In order to exude and communicate joy, you've got to smile. No one wants a "Debbie Downer" or "Angry Andy" selling them something. No one wants to meet up with someone who won't be smiling.

Selling is a transfer of emotion and smiling is the easiest way to do that. Think of this the next time you're having an argument with someone and step back and smile. When you smile, you instantly diffuse the situation.

I am so blessed with the people that I have been able to meet in my life just from a smile and to this day call friends. To me, the real fruit of success is never the money. It's never about the transaction. It's about the people you get to meet and the relationships that you create along the way.

"Don't cry because it's over. Smile because it happened."

~Dr. Seuss

Action Plan

_____

_____

_____

_____

_____

_____

_____

_____

_____

_____

_____

_____

_____

_____

_____

_____

_____

_____

RULE
#11
Pick Three Wins for the Day

When you think about winning, you can associate the momentum of the win with continued success. Winning is contagious. It has also become something that's expected. Once you win, you expect to win.

You can see it in professional team sports, when they hit a winning streak it creates momentum. The same momentum applies to losing. I want to give you a trick so that you can create your own winning momentum every single day. Get up every single day and pick three wins. This isn't meant to be insurmountable. You don't wake up and say, "I am going to climb Mount Everest." This is 3 simple things like:

I'm going to write a thank you note

I'm going to organize my files

I'm going to make that dreaded call that I don't want to make

Pick three simple things that are very achievable. Do this every day, for 30 days. If you do that every day, not just Monday through Friday, but every single day and create 3 wins for yourself, then after 30 days, you have 90 wins under your belt. You now have this incredible expectation that rolls you into the next month, "Alright, what am I going to win at now?" Great teams and great professionals expect to win. This trains you to expect to win. Not as an anomaly, "Oh wow, we won, isn't that unbelievable?!" NO! We expect to win!

This message isn't just for sales. Training yourself to win is applicable in all aspects of life, business, and even sports. My eldest son, Marc, was coaching at the University of Florida and he would occasionally talk about tidbits of stuff that I did with the team and the other coaches there at the University. I had posted one of my leadership presentations online and one of the guys on the Florida Staff had seen it. So, he wrote in their war room up on the wall, "Pick 3 wins for the day."

When my son Jake went to work at the University of Florida, over two years later, he headed into that war room and there it was, still on the wall. "Pick 3 wins for the day." Even at a college football level, choosing those 3 wins for the day can change your attitude and compound those wins over time, leading to more momentum in winning!

Your wins don't always have to pertain to your business, either. They could be about your life or who you are as a human being. It could even be stuff that you know needs to get done. Do you need to do things for your family? Do you need to clean your closet? Chase the wins. Life beats us up enough, create your own wins and watch how fast those wins start coming from everywhere. Then it becomes an expectation.

Your dominant thoughts and wins will create a new line of thinking. When you do that, you will see a change in your days. Why? Because you are training your mind to expect those wins. Your wins can be as simple as engaging with a stranger or volunteering to help someone else. When you invest in this simple step, you will start to conquer bigger and more significant wins with this change in mindset. You can call it a "must win list" rather than what everyone else calls it, a "to do" list.

"When you're that successful things have a momentum, and, at a certain point, you can't really tell whether you have created the momentum or it's creating you."

~Annie Lennox

Action Plan

_____

_____

_____

_____

_____

_____

_____

_____

_____

_____

_____

_____

_____

_____

_____

_____

_____

_____

RULE
#12

Luck Is For Those Who Are Unprepared

Do you know anyone who is successful? How do you think they got that way? Skill? Knowing the right people? Luck? People can get caught up in the idea that when others who get to be successful have done the right things and are making their way to the top, that it was luck. "You're so lucky!" "You made it to the top. You are the luckiest guy I know!"

If you want to be successful in sales, it has nothing to do with luck. People who show up in life and expect to get lucky will get slaughtered. When I have witnessed failure, I ask them, "What did you know about their business? What did you know about them? What did you know about the industry? What did you know about recent events that impacted the company?" All this information is easily accessible with social media and google. When I see people show up unprepared with that expectation to get lucky, those are the ones who fail.

Luck is for those that are unprepared. There are so many tools at my disposal, so much re-search and information that I can put together to be prepared. I can practice and do everything ahead of time. The thought that luck has anything to do with it is, completely, false.

Serial Entrepreneur, Gary Vanyerchuck says, "All of my friends from high school would call me and tell me, 'Gary you're so lucky!' and I would tell them, 'All that time when we were in college, and on Friday and Saturday when you went to the Jersey Shore and partied it up and were out with the girls, I worked.' Luck my ass. Don't tell me luck. Luck had nothing to do with it." Those that are successful will look back and say, "Did I have good fortune? Yes, but did I create the opportunity for me to have good fortune? YES!" It was not a game of chance.

"I really want this to happen." My pragmatic view is that, if you have done everything that you can do, if you have done the work, the rest will take care of itself. Do the best that you. Either it will happen or it won't. If you can look back and say, "I didn't do all that I could have done to make this successful," then you have created bad luck for yourself.

When my sales people leave for a visit and someone in our organization wishes them good luck, it will cost them $25 into the charity jar.

We have created a culture of owning outcomes and giving back at the same time. We don't need luck! Luck is for the unprepared!

Sales is not a game of chance. It isn't a board game and you aren't rolling dice to see if you get the sale or not. It is a well thought out intake and outtake of information. You are taking in the information and digesting it and then sending it back out and assessing what is going on through those interactions. Never wait on luck.

When my son Jake was 7, he went through a tough patch that most kids don't experience at that age. I sat him down and explained that life throws you curve balls. You have to learn to hit them. Now, if you ask him about curve balls and what that lesson taught him, he would say, "No matter what business or industry you are in or circumstance that life throws at you, you aren't always going to be ready for it. Curve balls can be tough to hit, but you can always learn to hit them and move on."

"When it comes to luck, you make your own."

~*Bruce Springsteen*

Action Plan

_____

_____

_____

_____

_____

_____

_____

_____

_____

_____

_____

_____

_____

_____

_____

_____

_____

_____

RULE
#13
Act Like It's Your First Day

Close your eyes and imagine the first day you went to work. Can you envision what you wore that day? Did you go to bed early? Did you map out the directions to drive there? How did you prepare?

I often ask people this question when I'm at a speaking engagement or consulting and it brings them back to a time when they were excited and passionate about what they do. Envision the night before your first day at work. You said to yourself, "I'll do whatever it takes to be successful." You were energetic and excited and ready to set the world on fire! You laid out your clothes and you plotted out your route to work. When you started out, you had no negative thoughts - anything was possible.

The longer you do what you do, the further away you get from that naiveté of, "I will do whatever it takes to be great." After 20 years, human nature doesn't allow you to do that. Now, it's very difficult to imagine that it's your first day. But, this rule is very important. In the beginning, you would do anything to be successful. If someone told you that the key to success was to go out back and wash their car, you would do it. You were open to learn; you would go out back and do it. You were open to new possibilities. When you think of that energy that you had that first day, all that negative behavior that happened over the years, goes away.

Think about an intern that comes into a company. Their specific job is to learn as much as they can. They are a sponge for the knowledge and training and, every single day they get up and go to work, they are excited to be there because of the opportunity they have to learn. Interns will do any job because they understand that being flexible will give them access to more opportunities to learn than being above any task.

When former NFL player Jerry Rice was asked why he was so successful, he answered, "I am willing to do things others won't."

If I told you to write down the things you did on that first day, what would you write?

"Oh, they made me make 100 phone calls."

"I had to file 6 months of reports."

"I picked up my CEO's dry cleaning and got his car cleaned."

On that first day, it didn't matter what they asked you to do. Why? Because the excitement of starting somewhere new and the inner goal to be successful no matter what, pushed you to do whatever it took. That drive is what gets us to that successful plateau. Evaluate how you became successful. History leaves clues, even your own history. All that can change when you follow this rule. **Act like it's your first day.**

*"Though no one can go back and make a brand new start,
anyone can start from now and make
a brand new ending."*

~Zig Ziglar

Action Plan

_____

_____

_____

_____

_____

_____

_____

_____

_____

_____

_____

_____

_____

_____

_____

_____

_____

_____

_____

RULE
#14
It's About Time

When I speak to sales people or entrepreneurs about time, they tell me one of the biggest struggles is time management. When I work with people they always tell me that they don't have time. "I would love to do that Steve, I just don't have time" or "That is a great suggestion Steve, but I don't have time to execute that."

Not having enough time is a fallacy. We all have time. In fact, we all have the exact same amount of time. Do you know how many seconds are in a day? 86,400 seconds. We all have the same clock. It is all about how we choose to use that time. How are you managing those 86,400 seconds? Time is so precious and, yet, so few people know anything about time. What if I waved a magic wand and gave you 7 hours more a week? What would you do with it? How would you spend those extra hours? This is a simple gift. You know how to do it? Get up an hour earlier!

How much time in the day do you have to dedicate to the things you want to do? There are 86,400 seconds in every day. Most people will say they don't have enough. Inevitably, when I coach people I say "Don't say you don't have enough time." The truth is that we all do. You are simply making a choice to do something you think is more important. You cannot make the excuse that you don't have time. If you look at your hours honestly, where are you dedicating your time? What is important to you? As Robin Sharma says, "What gets scheduled, gets done."

Now, it may be true that you're not managing your time. Consistency is the key here and, if you don't manage your time the same way you manage everything else, you're going to lose time without even knowing it. You'll find yourself at the end of a day wondering where time went.

Let's say you have $86,400 in the bank and someone stole $10 from you. Sure, you would be upset. But, you don't empty your account and burn the other $86,390 that you still have. You keep moving forward. Remember how many seconds we have in a day? 86,400. Would you let someone ruin the rest of your 86,390 seconds of your day that you still have over a bad 10 seconds? You didn't get back at anyone for spending your day engulfed in that negative 10 seconds.

In the movie In Time, time itself becomes money. Everyone in the film only ages to a maximum age of 25, or so, and the only way to stay alive is to earn, steal, or inherit more time. The population becomes a cast system of those who are hustling to earn new minutes for another day and those that have accumulated a wealth of stored up time. This system seems to work well until the lead actor, Justin Timberlake, finds a windfall of time that immediately gives him access to the world of the wealthy. Once there, he teams up with a beautiful young heiress and together they set out to destroy the corrupt system. However, the key in the movie is that because time is currency, people will do anything for it. Just like in our world today, where people will lie, cheat, steal, sell their souls, and rob others for money, in the film, some people do whatever it takes to get time. In one scene, bandits carjack a car to steal the time from the humans. Literally, time is currency and when it's gone—so are you. In our world today, people steal for money and, in that world, people steal time, buy time, and live each day fighting it or chasing it. It's a phenomenal film to illustrate the importance of time. We have only so much time and, the truth is, there's a race against the clock. What are we going to do with our time? How can I make the best of it? If you had more time what would you do?

I'd love to have more time to help people, to connect with family, or to create more opportunity. When sales people tell me they don't have enough time to prospect, I tell them it's a choice. The best sales people in the world have a lot of opportunity—but not because they have rich friends or more time - but because they create it.

If you wake up 1 hour earlier every day, that is 7 hours a week. After 30 days of doing that, you have gained a whole week! What could you accomplish with a week of your time back? How much more time could you dedicate to your family? This is why I get up at 3am! It impacts my life. I like it and I am living my life instead of sleeping it.

How well do you manage your time? This is another thing you have complete control over. Manage your time, your mind, and your life. You will see a huge improvement in your quality of life if you take responsibility over your time. An amazing friend of mine, Barry Gottlieb, who has been a trusted friend and advisor for me for many years knows it takes hard work, discipline, and continuous learning to be successful. He ends every event and blog post with, "Remember... Every day is a gift and the quality of your life is your gift to yourself."

Be intentional about your time and your results will increase. Time is a major issue for most sales professionals. Sometimes, when I go in to speak to a company, I'll address the sales team and say - "Sales is like shucking oysters. One out of every four are pearls." Sometimes you spend a lot of time on one single oyster and you may spend so much time on it but you may never get anywhere. Some sales people spend way too much time on people that shouldn't even be in their sales funnel. If you're in sales, that should resonate. How many times have you realized it was a wasted effort? That you shouldn't have taken the client or chased that lead?

We turn down clients all the time and, it's never easy but, it's always important. Once, I was on the phone with my team and a prospect and the prospect was nickel and diming us. I said to him, "Maybe this isn't the right time to work together." I wanted to get rid of it because I'd rather eliminate what could be a bad client than take on someone just to gain a win. A bad client isn't a win. Make your choices carefully. When you invest your time properly, similar to investing in the stock market, you can analyze and expect the right returns. We created a grid to help us evaluate these types of situations called The 4 Types of Client Relationships. Every prospect can fit into one of these four categories. Pay attention and you will steer clear from something we call the time vampires. People that suck the life and time out of your day.

The 4 Types of Client Relationships

Bad for you, bad for them

Good for you, bad for them

Bad for you, Good for them

Good for you, Good for them

When you think about time, just remember that you make a choice to do things that you believe are more important. You will make the time if it is important to you. So, create a routine. Make better choices. You are responsible for making those choices. You can choose to make a change or you can choose to continue keeping the same priorities. Success happens when you create systems for all the important areas of your life. When you do, you will find the results in each of these areas increasing.

"My favorite things in life don't cost any money. It's really clear that the most precious resource we all have is time."

~Steve Jobs

Action Plan

_____

_____

_____

_____

_____

_____

_____

_____

_____

_____

_____

_____

_____

_____

_____

_____

_____

_____

RULE
#15
Everyone Works From 8-5
Winners Work From 5-8

Everyone has this broad idea that, for most people, the work day is from 8-5pm. That is considered the traditional work day. I think working 8-5 is outdated. When you get out of that traditional mindset and you put people in a more relaxed environment, that is where the magic happens. The best opportunities happen either before the work day or after.

The world runs 24/7. The internet is the new printing press. It's the new library. It's the new database under no real controlling body. You can use it anywhere in the world at any time and that's what most of us use to do our jobs.

I get up every day at 3am to plan and execute my daily goals. By 8am, I am 5 hours ahead of everybody else. To do this, you must wake up early, wake up early, wake up early! Are you starting to get the message?

During the day, people get wrapped up in the things they need to do and don't have time to do the things that they want to do... (Like talking or engaging with you). Starting earlier or staying later helps you get more done.

I spent a few weeks playing email tag with a prospect and I wasn't getting any traction so, I sent him an email at 4am one morning on a Saturday. "I know we haven't been able to connect, how about breakfast Thursday morning?" At 4:20am, I got an email back that said "Absolutely." I know that busy professionals use before hours and after hours to be successful. They are not restricted to the 8-5pm.

Think about your own life and how busy you get during the day. How much different could you be between 5am-8am or 5pm-8pm? After 5pm, people let their guard down. Inviting someone out for a meal or "happy hour" is where the real relationship building begins. I have heard sales people say to me over and over "After 5pm is MY private time."

Mark Kaminsky, one of my lieutenants during the cellular phone days, learned that sales is not a job where you punch a clock. 5:00 - 8:00 or as I often refer to as... "bookends to success". Most people work in the comfort time of 8:00 - 5:00 because that is considered the norm; however, the highly successful work in both 3 hour blocks, when the norm is taking time off. The untold advantage is to be top of mind - first in of the day and last out of the day.

These rules don't live on an island. If you use them together you will see huge impacts in your relationships. I tell people to take the thirty-day challenge and do one thing they want to change for thirty days. Most people have a regret about how they spend their time. A lot of time is wasted. If you look back over your life, where would you say you wasted time and how could you change it? You can't get that lost time back but you can certainly influence the way you spend your time today.

"Give me six hours to chop down a tree and I will spend the first four sharpening the axe."

~Abraham Lincoln

Action Plan

_____

_____

_____

_____

_____

_____

_____

_____

_____

_____

_____

_____

_____

_____

_____

_____

_____

_____

RULE
#16
TGIS: The Grind Includes
Saturday and Sunday

We created TGIS as a movement. It stands for The Grind Includes Saturday and Sunday. This simply means, the extra effort that you put in on Saturday and Sunday, will pay big dividends.

Everyone has heard of TGIF - Thank God it's Friday. It's so popular, you will hear it every Friday. What's the difference between Friday and any other day? Really nothing.

I believe that's just an excuse to quit early, go into happy hour on Friday, and take the weekend off. If I get to work on Friday morning and my first thought is TGIF, I have already checked out for the day. Most people can't wait for the weekend! That's bullshit.

I coach people to think differently about their lives and business. Successful professionals are always thinking, even on weekends. CEO's think about their business day in and day out and you can bet they're thinking about their clients, processes, and vendors on Saturday and Sunday, as well.

People who live for Friday constantly complain about Monday. Monday has a bad reputation. But what if a Monday was the same as a Saturday? It's all about your attitude and mindset. For me, there's no difference between any of the days of the week. It is my choice on how to effectively use every day to accomplish the things that I want.

Remember, success leaves clues. Saturday and Sunday represent a time where you can get ahead of the pack, while others may be drinking, sleeping, and not doing any of the behaviors that push you towards success. This gives you an opportunity to take advantage of two extra days to connect and create relationships.

Envision your business life is like driving a car. Would you take your hands off the wheel for two days? Of course, you wouldn't! You wouldn't want to cause an accident or worse. So, why would you do that for your business? You can't leave for two days and expect to come back on Monday and be successful.

Successful professionals understand that parties, neighborhood barbecues, and fun events are still a time to meet, greet, and develop relationships. In fact, Michael Dublin, creator of the Dollar Shave

Club, created his business on a Saturday night at a party when he was asked to move a warehouse full of razor blades. He just recently sold his company for 1 Billion dollars. That isn't a typo. If he chose to work only from 8-5 and dismissed the business opportunity without a thought because of what day it was, he wouldn't have just sold his company for 10 figures. Chances to create and grow your business happen at all hours. Not just 8-5.

Enterprise Holdings is a client of mine. We were doing training for them in New Jersey and New York. I gave the presentation to 100 people and, every time I finish a presentation, I ask what the #1 take away was for each of them. One guy said, "I am going try this TGIS thing." So, fast forward a week, I get an email from him, "Hey, your presentation was great. I told you I was, specifically, going to do this TGIS thing and, I have."

Remember, in the previous chapter, the email I sent that early Saturday morning? Not only did I get an email back, he said I could call him at that moment. Imagine that! Be assertive and expect to win. I had a definitive, relationship-moving conversation that day! On a Saturday.

TGIS is a mindset. It's a way to live and work, and a way to continue those relationships that can lead to more connections and, possibly, more sales. It is a win-win. Don't let go of the wheel for two days! Remember, the rule about waking up early? This concept gives you two days ahead of the game on your competition. If other sales teams are taking the weekend off, you now have the chance to get up early on Saturday and kill it. You have two days ahead of the business week so, use it to create more relationships and connections. Don't limit your work life to the weekdays.

"If you do what you love, you'll never work a day in your life."

~Marc Anthony

Action Plan

_____

_____

_____

_____

_____

_____

_____

_____

_____

_____

_____

_____

_____

_____

_____

_____

_____

_____

_____

RULE
#17
Let's Get Social

How has social media impacted our sales environment? In today's world, social media is about transparency and connectivity. It offers you the ability to research, learn, and know who someone is even before you contact them. You get to see their likes, their dislikes, and the things they post about. All you've got to do is spend time researching! This is about preparation and connectivity. They call it "social" media because it is supposed to be social and social is fun!

Social media is a broadcast channel. Similar to the 800+ channels that we get on our TVs, everyone one of those channels is programmed with unique content. In this case, your social media channel is your opportunity to broadcast all the things that you want people to know about you. Social media allows us to both listen and talk. While we can find out so much about a prospect or a client through social media, we can also educate others about who we are, what we do, and what we are passionate about.

I had a prospective client come to me about creating a training program for them. I went to visit their company and check out their sales floor to get an idea of how their sales team was functioning so I could better visualize how their training system would best serve them. I had them give me an example of a sales prospect they were working on. They were trying to reach out to the Director of Marketing, multiple times, with no success. The prospect was going to be moved to the dead file. I asked them, "What kind of research have you done on the Director of Marketing?" "None" was the answer. "What kind of research have you done on the company and what their initiatives are?" "None." "What's their charity of choice?" "We don't know."

So, together we did some research. We went directly to LinkedIn and researched the company as well as the individuals who worked there. We made a discovery that the director of marketing (who they were trying to contact) was recently married and now had a hyphenated last name. They were trying to connect with her through the wrong name. We also found out that she went to University of North Carolina. Her LinkedIn page showed she was part of many alumni groups, as is common with people that attend the University of North Carolina. We made the assumption that she was a huge basketball fan. Equipped with this knowledge, we had the sales rep contact the prospect next time North Carolina wins a game. I said, "When they win, email her and say, 'Congratulations on the win! Go Blue!'"

She got instant engagement from the other side. Just by knowing something important about her prospect, it changed the perspective from the classic, "Hi, I am here to interrupt your day so that I can sell you" to "I want to connect with you about something I know is important to you." Can you see the difference this will make in your relationships? Social media is a huge tool that you can use to learn more about the people that you want to engage with!

Being social is an investment of time and thought and the information that you receive brings you very close to success. Updating your Facebook page isn't enough. Making a post or sending a tweet isn't enough. Authentically connect! Ask people how they are, ask how their kids are, and find out what's important to them. It will transform the relationships you have and you will have more ways to connect with prospects than you thought possible.

I was hired by an employee benefits company to come in and coach their team. In speaking to their top sales guy, he said to me that he only wanted to do business with CEO's that play golf. I looked at him and I said, "When you are done smoking the whacky weed, let's have a serious conversation. You can't seriously only market to CEO's that play golf." I was not going to even entertain the conversation. A couple days later, I called him and said, "I thought about it. What would happen if you could do that? What would happen if you only speak to CEO's that play golf and love golf?" This sales guy was a scratch golfer (A **"scratch golfer"** is a player who can play to a Course Handicap of zero on any, and all, rated golf courses. A male **scratch golfer,** for rating purposes, can hit tee shots an average of 250 yards and can reach a 470-yard hole in two shots at sea level.) He is going to be able to have very relevant conversations with golfers because he speaks their same language. He can train them on golf and he can train their kids. Through the bond that they create about golf, they will, ultimately, have the opportunity to discuss business. **It is all about gaining trust and credibility.**

He had access to his entire golf club and we decided to do a golf event 8 times a year, strictly so he could meet CEO's who love golf. Together with Rich Rogers, the founder, we named the event 6 Degrees of Golf with the tagline, "Business is a Contact Sport." That event still goes on every other month. The amount of business and great relationships that have been attributed to that event is incredible. It proved to me that, whatever your passion is, golf, fishing, sports, whatever, if you align yourself with people who have like passions, the world changes.

Today, companies have organized, well-staffed, procurement

organizations with specific objectives of selecting products using unbiased and budget-oriented methodologies. Sophisticated, cross-functional, procurement teams, often using complex scoring and evaluation techniques, are poised to review products and services from several providers. Even with the popularity of these systems and processes, relationships become even more critical and sometimes the only significant way to differentiate your selling organization, your product, and your company.

Today, the new reality of selling is relationship selling. Relationship selling is focused on being able to consistently communicate across all possible channels, authentically engaging with clients while intently listening to uncover their needs and issues. Hence the name "social media".

Social media is here to stay. There is a huge dance party going on. Who has fun at dance parties? The people who dance! You have to get on the dance floor. People who stand against the wall don't have a good time. I have reconnected with so many people through social media that I may never have had the opportunity to connect with if social media didn't exist. It has created refreshed relationships that can lead to new business possibilities. Face to face is important and meaningful. But, deep relationships are built on consistent conversations and sales are built on relationships. Get yourself and your message out there! Tell the world!

"The incredible brand awareness and bottom-line profits achievable through social media marketing require hustle, heart, sincerity, constant engagement, long-term commitment, and most of all, artful and strategic storytelling."

~Gary Vaynerchuk

Action Plan

_____

_____

_____

_____

_____

_____

_____

_____

_____

_____

_____

_____

_____

_____

_____

_____

_____

_____

RULE
#18
Sell or Be Sold

There's a dance going on in every conversation—someone is selling and someone is being sold. The sooner you realize this the more successful you will be. Are you selling or are you being sold?

I want salespeople to think of every single dialogue. If the prospective client said, "We just don't have the budget for it", I say that could be bullshit. If you said you're going to cure cancer, they'd have the budget for it. What can you do differently? Figure out a different way.

Everybody is selling something all the time and the faster you realize this, the faster you will be able to take control of the conversation. I am a student of the game. I chose to breakdown all the pieces of every dialogue. For those of you that have kids, think about the last time you told your kid they needed to go to bed. You let them know it was 8pm and it was bedtime and they start saying, "Can't I stay up a little later? Please, just to finish this game?" Who is selling who? When was the last time you went into a restaurant and the maître' d told you they didn't have any tables? Who is selling who?

During the holidays, I visited one of my favorite restaurants and was told we couldn't be seated for an hour and a half. I could have taken what she said at face value and have either waited or left to find someplace with a shorter wait. Instead, I changed the dance by suggesting to her that I am a top client, that I am there even when they are not busy, and if there was any way she could accommodate us. Within ten minutes, she had seated my party of six. All of this illustrates similar to Fred Astaire and Ginger Rogers - when they were dancing, someone was leading.

In sales, you need to understand the nature of every conversation and lead it to where you want it to go. The next time someone says, they don't have the budget or the time, think about what your next step would be to lead the dance.

"The best way to sell yourself to others is first to sell the others to yourself."

~Napoleon Hill

Action Plan

_____

_____

_____

_____

_____

_____

_____

_____

_____

_____

_____

_____

_____

_____

_____

RULE
#19
Practice Makes Perfect

To become an expert at something, how many hours do you think you need to practice at it? A week? A month? It takes 10,000 hours of practice for you to become an expert at something.

Think about the Super Bowl. The two competing teams spend the two weeks before the major game doing what? They practice. They practice the same plays over and over. In baseball, every spring, the players get together to practice. It is all about the fundamentals: hitting, throwing, running, and practicing!

When the Patriots won the Super Bowl in 2015, in the final play of the game, Malcom Butler intercepted a pass that won them the game. When the game was over and they interviewed him, they asked, "That was an amazing catch and an amazing play! How did you do that?" Butler said, "Honestly, Coach Belichick had us practice that exact play 4 million times. I saw the play ten steps before it happened. It was all about the practice." The final play in the game was important because Butler saw the formation and reacted to what they had practiced over and over. Because of that practice, he was prepared for it. The practice was the reason he was able to intercept the ball and win the game. **Practice!**

Sales is as strong a profession as your friends who are doctors and lawyers. But for some reason, when you ask somebody what they think of salespeople, what do they normally think of? Used cars! It's okay. You can say it. When it comes to sales people, and them telling people what they do, very few of them practice their response. A great place to practice, is how to answer the question, "What do you do?"

Ask people the question, "What do you do?" and they will say, "I sell insurance.", "I'm a mortgage broker.", "I'm a salesman.", or "I'm a doctor or a lawyer." That's part of what you do but it's not who you are. I sell who I am. Always. Lead with that first. It's not really a transaction at all. I am motivated by providing value. If I provide enough value, the right ones around will stick around. I'm a connector and I love people. If I can sell things based on being my authentic self, life is good.

Figure out your personal mission statement. Your "Why". Practice in front of a mirror. The team at OnFire Books creates legacy books and coaches leaders on their brand and platform. If you ask them what they do, they don't say, "We write books." They would tell you that they are driven to help leaders create incredible legacies through words. This is a very different way to describe what you do. You must be intentional about your why and about how you communicate that with the people you connect with. Practice it! It is about a specific, deliberate action. You are creating muscle memory and instinct. People practice so they can capture what works and remove what doesn't.

*"Practice does not make perfect.
Only perfect practice makes perfect."*

~Vince Lombardi

Action Plan

_____

_____

_____

_____

_____

_____

_____

_____

_____

_____

_____

_____

_____

_____

_____

_____

_____

_____

RULE
#20
Networking Is Only One Letter Away from Not Working

To be good in sales and in life, you have to be good at networking. But, where people get it wrong is that they see networking as an event. Networking is not an event, it's a lifestyle.

Some of the best networking I have done is in casual conversations that happened before or after the "networking" event. If you are living in the "networking is an event" mindset, you are going to miss all the other opportunities.

Some of the best deals I have done came from when I was sitting in the airport waiting on a flight. That is where I have met some of the most interesting people. As I mentioned before, I am genuinely curious about other people. One time, I met a gentleman on a plane from Idaho, Daniel Krancer. He was from a company called Power Engineers. I always live in connect mode. I was curious about who he was, what he did, and what makes him tick. We had a great time "visiting" with each other while we were on the plane and it made the flight seem to go very fast. When we landed in Atlanta, I invited him to the Delta Club. I told him, "I got this man. It's my pleasure." It was $25 and it gave us the chance to talk over drinks. We then got connected on all of the social media channels and we make it a point to stay in touch. A couple of weeks later, I get a message from him that says, "Hey, I have been watching you on social media and I see the training and speaking you are doing and I would love to talk to you about an opportunity with my company in Idaho." I got that opportunity because I was "networking" on the plane.

It is about developing relationships that lead to business opportunities. Whether they buy from you or not is irrelevant. They now know what you do. Networking is not a defined event and too many sales people live their lives thinking that is exactly what it is.

Think about all the situations where you can network. Can you network at church or temple? Yes. Can you network while your kid is at soccer practice? Yes. Understanding what networking is and, the power of it, is crucial.

Networking is about doing the work. You must have undying faith that if you do enough of the work, the results will be there. It's hard work! Be intentional and don't give up because there's a pearl in there somewhere. I am genuinely curious so, it's authentic. But, there's still a lot of work in opening opportunities.

If I told a room of 100 people that each of them had to go out today, close a deal, and make something happen today or they get fired, how many people do you think would be successful? 90% of them will get fired. Someone could get lucky (which I don't believe in). They may close a deal - may not be a good deal but they would be on the short list of people who didn't get fired. Change it up. What if I told that same room of people to go out and make 5 new friends? How many people do you think could be successful? 100%.

Doug Jackson was the CMO for a dotcom start-up called Z-Tel Technologies in Tampa, FL. I was building and growing On the Ball. I had cold-called Doug and asked if I could fly up, (on my own dime), to better understand their marketing needs and determine if I might be a good fit and provide value for his emerging brand. About a week later, I showed up at Doug's desk and the rest is history. Doug said, "Steve was a master of maintaining a great attitude and persistently coming back with new, fresh ideas that always reflected our feedback. Ultimately, he became our go-to source for marketing and promotional efforts, was a fixture within our company, and we've been working together ever since. Suffice it to say; 18 years, 1 Super Bowl, countless projects, numerous road trips, innumerable cigars and cocktails later – Steve is still one of my best friends on earth and that boundless energy, curiosity, and enthusiasm that he had 18 years ago, continues to drive him today." That is being "on the ball."

When you play Bingo, and you have more cards on the table, you have more opportunity for success. The more relationships you have, the more opportunity you have to create business opportunities. Most sales people focus on the result not on the process. The process is all about the people. Focus on the process! You will have a richer life, you will meet and engage with wonderful people who add value to your life, and that, ultimately, will buy from you or they will refer you to someone who will.

"You can make more friends in two months by becoming interested in other people than you can in two years by trying to get other people interested in you."

~Dale Carnegie

Action Plan

_____

_____

_____

_____

_____

_____

_____

_____

_____

_____

_____

_____

_____

_____

_____

_____

_____

_____

RULE
#21
Tell Me Something Good

Have you ever heard the song by Rufus & Chaka Khan "Tell Me Something Good"? It debuted in 1974 and spent a week as the number one song in the Cash Box Top 100. Since then, several bands have covered the song from Dave Matthews to Pink.

I believe it was a hit because everyone wants something good in a world of negativity. I use this song to start every single one of my conversations. Why? As human beings, we are trained to ask, "How are you?" It's an open-ended question that gives people the opportunity to take the negative junk they have been carrying and give that weight to you. They want to give you all their negatives. As a sales person, you are starting out in a ditch. How can they pay attention to you and your message if they are already focused on their negative story? Why put them in a position to offer up a problem? The normal dialogue goes like this - "Hey Bob, how are you?" "Oh Steve, it's terrible! My job sucks and I hate my boss!" People who continually do that are unintentional with their words. Now, you have to come back and get them back from their negative thoughts in order to get anywhere positive.

What if there was a different way? Instead, I coach sales teams to open with a positive sentence. Let's guide the conversation in a positive direction. I say, "Hello Darlene, Tell me something good!" "Steve, my son just finished his second semester at MIT! We are so proud of him." Just then, I said, "Tell me more." Once she had finished, she responded back with, "Why don't you tell me something good, Steve?" See the difference in the exchange of conversation? Change the dialogue from "How are you?" to "Tell me something good."

First, they will be dumbfounded. Second, whatever they say that makes them feel good, focus on that. You can also now steer the conversation because we are in a good state of mind. We have created a solid base for receiving information.

This song will stay with you forever. It is just another example of the power of music. You will think of this song, hum it, and it will help you remember to start things off with, "Tell me something good!"

"Keep your face to the sunshine and you cannot see a shadow."

~Helen Keller

Action Plan

RULE
#22
It's All About the Words

If you're going to be really, really successful in life, you'll need to focus on your vocabulary. Words are everything. The words you say to yourself and, of course, others are very important to your success. We talk worse to ourselves than we would ever let anyone talk to us.

Words matter. The word **win** is a word that doesn't mean what people think. Most people think that win is about either winning or losing. It's really about "what's important now?" I learned this from the great, college football coach, Nick Saban. "If you lose a game, or you have a bad play, most people will focus on what went wrong rather than what is happening during that second. Specifically, in football, a new play happens every 40 seconds. You can't worry about the future." In boxing, if you get knocked down, you have 10 seconds to get up. What is important in that moment during that situation? It is right now that is important. For sales people, these are very significant lessons on focus. Most sales people are still dejected about a deal they lost long ago, and that affects their ability to be in the now. Don't forget to focus on **WIN.** Not the past and not the future but now.

Now, I am going to give you the best 3 words in sales. And they are **Visit, Fit,** and **Value.** First, the most powerful word in sales is visit. It is common practice to evaluate sales teams based on the amount of appointments they have. I don't like the word appointments. You make an appointment with your doctor or your dentist and even the DMV. Why would sales people try to make appointments with their prospects? Same thing goes for the word meeting. By shifting meetings and appointments to **visits,** you will see incredible results. Think about the last time you visited with a friend. Did you bring brochures? Did you sit across from each other at your desk? Think about what you talked about? Visiting is a friendly way to interact with people. It reminds people of a good occasion.

This next word is the game changer. Want to change the paradigm of selling? This is the second most powerful word in sales – **Fit.** I shift the control in the dialogue straight from the beginning on that first call. "The reason for my **visit,** is to determine if we are a good **fit.**" Visiting and understanding who is a fit will take control of the sales dance again placing you as the lead. Now, just because you want to buy from me doesn't mean I have to say yes. The control has gone from the buyer to the sales person. Human nature is that people want to "fit in". They want to be part of things. You changed their mind set to "Why wouldn't I be a good fit for you?"

If you don't take control of the dance in sales, then you will lose. Authentically, know your work. Know who you are. Let people know that you have an exclusivity mindset and we may not be the business or product for you. You may not buy from me. And that is ok. It is a shift from the puppy dog sales person who is, "Please buy from me, please buy from me." Not begging for the sale brings down their guard because people don't like to say no. There was an advertising campaign done, years ago, by American Express. The campaign was a series of commercials that pinpointed all the ways that being a card holder had special benefits. Their tagline? Membership has its privileges.

When you stop using the begging sales person as your motto, you realize that exclusivity in your sales, in your business, and in your life is a game-changer. You create that club. Everyone wants to be part of a club that they can't get in.

So, we have **visit** and **fit.** What is the final word that will change the way you operate? **Value.** Now we are visiting to see if we are a fit. If we are a fit, then we can about talk about how we can provide **value.**

There is never a sale that is made if you can't deliver value. Most sales people don't con-sider the value portion of their sales equation. If they heard no, chances are they haven't created enough value. Have you solved a problem? What is the value you are offering that will improve, over and above, what they are already doing? Value is at the crux of every single sales conversa-tion. "I want to deliver **value** to you, just like I do for Enterprise or Bank United." Now you have thrown in some social credibility. "You do business with Bank United? I want to get into that club."

I don't care what product you are selling, what price you are selling it for, or what business you are in. This works across all industries. Let's set up a **visit** so, we can find out if we are a **fit** and, if we are then I can provide you with **value**.

The challenge is to start every dialogue with these 3 words. Get as many **visits** as you can to see if you are a **fit** to see if you can provide **value**.

"Watch your thoughts, they become your words.
Watch your words, they become your actions.
Watch your actions, they become your habits.
Watch your habits, they become your character.
Watch your character, it becomes your destiny."

~Anonymous

Action Plan

_____

_____

_____

_____

_____

_____

_____

_____

_____

_____

_____

_____

_____

_____

_____

_____

_____

RULE
#23
The Paul Revere Method

Many sales people have a narrow focus on their target market. But sales is a numbers game. The more people you know, the more opportunity you have.

When we work with sales teams, I always evaluate how they prospect first. In most cases, they have established a target audience like CFO's, and then all their efforts are aimed at that group of people. I ask, "Who is your target market?" Let's say they answer with, "We target CFO's of companies that have more than 50 employees." I'll ask, "That's pretty specific. Where do you spend your activities?" The client usually replies with something like, "I exclusively spend my time with CFO's of companies with more than 50 employees." But, if I can get them to widen their target, their success will increase.

Sales is a numbers game. Think about this. If you target only this market, you are leaving out so many people that may be a friend, a colleague, a relative, or simply be 1 degree away. Who else knows CFO's? Those are the people who you need to know. Do accountants and tax organizations know CFO's? Do CEO's? How about entrepreneurs or COO's? Presidents and Vice Presidents? Every one of those contacts is going to know someone who could be an amazing new relationship.

We all know who Paul Revere is, right? He didn't just ride around telling a few people the British were coming. He shouted it to everyone! Sales people need to tell everyone their story. I've said this before but, I always ask sales people "when you drive up to your house and walk in the door and your neighbor sees you, do they know what you do?" Even those relationships matter. It isn't about what you do, it's about who you know. Even if it's your neighbor, your kid's teacher, or their football coach. You never know who will know someone that needs whatever it is you provide!

The more quality visits you are on, the more powerful your results. So, I believe there is no such thing as a bad visit. How can time spent with someone talking about your business be bad? Great sales people invest in relationships. Every visit means connecting and building on a relationship that could lead somewhere in the future. Say you connected with a company about your software management system and maybe you aren't a good fit for them now because they are still growing. If you maintain that relationship, they may know a larger company that could use your services. Or, when they grow, they may call you first when they are ready to make that upgrade.

Be genuine and understand that there's a lot you can learn from every-one. When you've got that point of view you will never look at an individual as a means-to-an-end but a relationship instead. There is value in every relationship. If the object of every visit is to inform and educate people on what you are looking for in your business, (training them to be a sales look out for you) your business will explode.

"We're so complex; we're mysteries to ourselves; we're difficult to each other. And then storytelling reminds us we're all the same."

~Brad Pitt

Action Plan

_____

_____

_____

_____

_____

_____

_____

_____

_____

_____

_____

_____

_____

_____

_____

_____

_____

RULE
#24
Listen Up

"The most basic and powerful way to connect to another person is to listen. Just listen. Perhaps the most important thing we ever give each other is our attention." Rachel Naomi Remen

Most people hear; they just don't listen. Hearing refers to the sounds that enter your ears. It is a physical process that happens automatically. Listening, however, requires more than that. It requires focused and concentrated effort, both mental and, sometimes, physical, as well. Research suggests that we remember between 25 to 50 percent of what we hear. That means that when you talk to your boss, colleagues, customers, or spouse for 10 minutes, they pay attention to less than half of the conversation!

In fact, Public speaking is a coveted business skill, and has specific groups like Toastmasters that offer skill development, while listening is virtually ignored. Think about this for a minute - most people do not listen with the intent to understand; they listen with the intent to reply. Most people are thinking more about what they want to say rather than what someone else is saying. It happens and we are all guilty of it.

Conversation is a lot like playing tennis…there is a constant volley going on. Great sales people are acutely aware of this volley. When the ball is in your court, (speaking) you serve up your words. When it is not, you need to be paying attention to the words of others. Not the only what they are saying but how they are saying it, how loud, how much passion etc.… How are they telling their story? What is their use of language and voice and what is their body language saying? In other words, it means being aware of both verbal and non-verbal messages and cues.

Your ability to listen effectively depends on the degree to which you perceive and under-stand these messages. Epictetus once said, "We have two ears and one mouth so that we can listen twice as much as we speak."

As a student of the sales game, I have trained myself to gather as much information as pos-sible, in an effort, to build genuine relationships. Everyone wants to be heard and understood, and the reward is the trust and loyalty from those around us. Asking open ended questions, ones that cannot be answered by yes or no, are key to gaining this trust.

For me, I only need to ask one question and I sit back and intently listen when I ask "What's your story....?" You have created a simple and effective way to get people talking. Now, all you need to do is be fully present and in the moment and just listen.

There is a new way that we need to learn to listen. Social listening. With the world of social media, there is more talking going on. Paying attention to social media, and being socially aware of the clues being posted, can give you a way to be very effective in communicating in a way that is mandatory in all areas of life.

To be effective, you will need to listen, observe, and understand people's wants, needs, and likes through all the various ways that you communicate with them. Whether that is at a visit, through email, a call, or connecting on social media, these are key so you can then begin building relationships on a foundation of trust and communication.

Regardless of the outcome, some of the very best relationships I have, today, are with those contacts that have never bought a thing from me.

"The art of conversation lies in listening."

~Malcom Forbes

Action Plan

_____

_____

_____

_____

_____

_____

_____

_____

_____

_____

_____

_____

_____

_____

_____

_____

_____

RULE
#25
Follow Up

What is the proper time frame to follow up with someone? 48 hours? A week? Think about someone you met last week. If you wait too long, it is unlikely they will remember much about you. Follow up is part of the process for success. Follow up, immediately!

For most professional contacts, it takes about 6-7 conversations with someone you meet through networking for a professional relationship to form. 80% of deals need at least 5 touches before closing, so keeping the conversation alive is an indispensable skill.

People buy when they're ready to buy, not when you're ready to sell. This is huge.

Follow up means staying top of mind with your audience so that you can be in front of folks when they're ready to buy. In other words, you must follow up with them regularly, not just after the first encounter.

When you say you will follow up, do it! This is one way you can demonstrate you are a person who keeps their word.

It is unbelievable how many people NEVER follow up. Something simple, short, and sweet works every time. You should "touch" every potential opportunity in your pipeline by sending relevant and valuable information regularly, relentlessly, and frequently. There are so many tools to use: phone, email, direct mail, social media, invites to events, etc. Use the tools you have and mix it up. Every contact you have is going to have a preferred method of communication.

If every follow up is about business though, how are you showing your prospect that you care about them? Follow up about birthdays, anniversaries, family events, milestones, community events, vacations, or even business deals they may have shared with you.

Follow up has to be genuine, every time. Let's say you and I had a great conversation. Why would I waste any time following up? Why wouldn't I just send you an email now? I have all the tools in my hand. When you do, you send the message that they are important and you haven't even done business, yet. You create the impression in their mind that, "Wow. This is how fast he followed up and we haven't done business yet. How fast will he follow up when we do business?" If we wait 48 hours, or even the next day, chances are, you will forget or push it off.

That is a lost opportunity. And for what? Waiting some randomly generated moment that you think you have time to connect back?

In the movie Swingers, Vince Vaughn says he always waits 6 days before calling a girl after a date. If life is like one big dating game, as I see it, then how long should people wait to get in touch after a first date, a first visit, or a first encounter. There are an endless number of sales prospects. In that sea of prospects, how important do you treat each, and every, relationship? Follow up is a discipline that you set in your mind. How important to you is that second or third touch? Should you follow up in a week? A month? Most sales people haven't created a system for those prospects. Follow up is generally random and that is a big mistake! That is where most people lose their traction.

You can make a huge impact just by creating a system for following up. If the last person that you spoke with told you they were going skiing with their family that weekend, you would be taking notes (Rule #7 Read and Write) and you will be able to follow up next week and ask, "Hey, how was your ski trip?"

It's one of the keys to success. With so many ways to communicate: calling, texting, emailing, Facebook, etc., you need to create your strategy and stick to a consistent game plan! No matter when you do it, make it consistent. My plan has always been to follow up any interaction before the start of the next day. It is another reason why I get (yet, another reason) up early.

This is a game changer. Ask a real relationship question; just as you would do with a friend, you should do with a prospect. These things represent who you are. It doesn't matter about the sale or how they respond. You do this with every client and the right things will happen. When you do it randomly then you don't know who you might miss.

Don't make the mistake of not following up. Be disciplined and do those little things that develop those relationships. Think about this - you aren't bad because you didn't follow up, you are better because you did.

"The way we communicate with others and with ourselves ultimately determines the quality of our lives."

~Tony Robbins

Action Plan

_____

_____

_____

_____

_____

_____

_____

_____

_____

_____

_____

_____

_____

_____

_____

_____

_____

_____

_____

RULE
#26
3D PR – Emotional Intelligence

Most people know what PR is. PR is a way companies tell their story through different media outlets, including their reps. As sales people, we have been trained to sell our company first.

For years, the name on the building was more important than the person. "My name is Steve, and I represent On the Ball." But, the reality is that your personal brand matters more because it's the bridge between two corporations.

Let's say, I am trying to sell On the Ball to Toshiba. In reality, those two brands don't interact. It is how my personal brand interacts with you, as the decision maker, that matters. The decision maker is more important than the company in the sense that, if I create a relationship with the decision maker, then, I have a shot at working with the company.

3D PR gives you a chance to market directly to a person as opposed to the company. When you begin to look at life and business in this way, it removes the questions and the complexity because you can see that it's truly all about human interaction. The quality of your relationships will determine the trajectory of your success in sales.

On one particular sales trip, we flew to Cleveland and we were working with the Reps there on one of the opportunities they were going after. The decision maker was unresponsive. They had communicated through email and phone calls with no success. I asked them how long they had been trying to connect and they said 3 months. I asked, "At what point are you going to say to yourself that this strategy isn't working? They are not going to respond to you. They don't know you. What is the next step?"

I told the team that we were going to use a 3D PR strategy. We are going to make the PR part of this come to life. We are going to use emotional intelligence. We are going to find out something about the person instead of the company.

We did some online research and found out that the guy they had been unable to connect with was a huge James Bond fan. We purchased a James Bond martini shaker from Amazon and created a hand-written note that said, "Hey, we have been trying to connect with you for a while. All we want is the opportunity to shake things up."

Lo and behold, the guy responded!

Think about this. When you send a package like this to the office, the receptionist signs for it and says, "Hey Sam, you have a package." Now everyone in the office is interested in what is in that box. Sam opens the box, "Wow, that is really cool!" He is surprised and impressed by something this thought out. Now, everyone in the office sees that Sam got this awesome package and what did it do? It is a clever marketing tool. The decision maker, now, wonders how you knew he loved James Bond. How did they make that reference? It is a 3D package that opens up the decision makers heart, and now the chances of you getting that face-to-face meeting is significantly higher.

The decision maker has a huge impact on how you do business and sell to any company. If you can't find information as specific as James Bond, remember that everyone on LinkedIn has the college they graduated from listed. Most sales people don't think about this because they are too busy marketing to the company instead of the person. With 3D PR, it's a personal approach and it allows you to open doors immediately. You are taking what is important to the decision maker and marketing to them instead of the company.

In any sales opportunity, you can go on social media and find out where the decision maker went to college. Let's say they went to the University of Florida. I purchase a University of Florida basketball and we drop a note in there, "Hey, we noticed you're a Gator. We just want the opportunity to get the ball rolling."

If I sent you a basketball from the college that you graduated from with that message, you would probably open the doors to communication instantly. You are preparing their hearts for the relationship building that will either result in a sale, or result in a connection that can lead to more relationships and sales in the future. It is about emotional intelligence. What is important to you? What is important to the decision maker? Use that in a way that is 3D and emotionally intelligent and you will open doors that have been locked to connecting.

When I started On the Ball, 25 plus years ago, I went to Sports Authority and I purchased bases. Yes, actual bases that you would run in baseball. We printed the definition of first base, tacked it to the base, and added a hand-written note. The definition of first base, 3rd down in the dictionary says, "A first meeting." We handpicked 25 decision makers in the market place and sent the bases to each of them.

Here is the difference in these decision makers. We didn't choose 25 that we wanted to buy from us. We chose 25 that we wanted to know who we were. The marketing ploy: "We just want to get to first base with you." We got 25 call backs. Not 25 sales. This is how you build relationships. In fact, one of those relationships, Salomon Sredni, continues to refer business to On the Ball to this very day.

Be creative and authentic in your strategy and you will reach people in a way that is unforgettable. They may not buy from you, but they won't forget you. That relationship could be what connects you to someone who WILL buy from you. It's always about relationships.

Creativity opens doors that may have otherwise stayed closed. 3D PR isn't just for sales or business. Remember, we are all selling something. Mike Tomlinson at Toshiba recently called me to share his daughter, Melanie's, success.

"Steve, I took your 3D PR and shared it with my daughter. She has been working on getting noticed for softball at a collegiate level. Coaches are contacted by hundreds of students from around the region to play for these schools and to get their attention; creativity is important. I suggested she use 3D PR to connect with the coaches of these schools. For a catcher, one of the important strengths is throwing ability and quickness for throwing out base runners. This is called and measured as the "Pop Time" from home plate to second base and this exhibits the strength of a catcher. She played off the "pop" and sent each school a popcorn bucket with Pop Secret Popcorn in them. Her tagline: 'My Pop time should not be a secret, so I thought I would share it with you.' She not only got noticed, but was offered a full scholarship. 3D PR as a marketing tool is effective and will capture the attention of your target audience."

As a sales person, you must have a shift in mentality. Instead of you sending something about you, send them something about them. If it's always about the customer or prospect, how can a conversation get sideways? People love talking about their interests. Find out what they are. This is a fool proof way to connect on an emotional level with not just the decision maker, but with the company. I can hear you asking me, "What if they don't respond?" It is simple. Cross them off your list. If they don't respond to something like this, then move forward. Selling is built on relationships!

"I've learned that people will forget what you said, people will forget what you did, but people will never forget how you made them feel."

~Maya Angelou

Action Plan

_____

_____

_____

_____

_____

_____

_____

_____

_____

_____

_____

_____

_____

_____

_____

_____

_____

_____

_____

RULE
#*27*
Give to Get

Every sales manager programs their sales team, right at the start, to go GET the business and GET the sale. Change that mindset to GIVE first.

Giving means a lot of different things. It could mean joining a charity board and giving your time. Why do this? Who's on charity boards? CEO's, Entrepreneurs, and business owners. Everyone that you want to do business with is already involved with a charity of their choice. These are the people you need to connect with! Giving your time will get you tremendous results.

In changing this mindset, go into your next visit and, instead of thinking about what you are going to sell them, think about what you are going to give them and who you are going to connect them with. Sit down with them and listen to them talk about their business and say, "You know there are 3 people that you need to connect with that could use your business services tomorrow." You will get their business instantly and they will never leave. Why? Because there are no vendors that give. They are just looking to take.

Ask the question, "How can I be of service to you?" Think beyond selling them something. How are you operating? When you go into that visit with a client, are you there to help build their business or just your own?

What has changed the game for me is that I don't think of who I can sell. I think of how I can give. In every networking conversation, every waking minute that I can, I am thinking of ways I can give. The more you give, the more you get. This is a fundamental rule. Giving your time, your money, or mentoring, will make you a better person.

You need to be willing to reset your mind and say, "I have a process here that can make my life better." If you shift the focus from you to them, you will have a better life. Not just a better sales life, or business life. A better life in every aspect.

Duane Cummings, the CEO of Leadercast, a Co-Founder of The Speakers Guild of America, and Founder of The Sensational Group LLC., said it best, "I truly want to die empty. That would come from giving myself away. Sharing all my experience, knowledge, gifts, and talents. The funny thing is that old rule about the more you give the more you receive is so true. So, although my goal is to give myself away, I continued to be filled up, renewed, refreshed, and the cycle or opportunity gets bigger every day."

"We make a living by what we get.
We make a life by what we give."

~Winston Churchill

Action Plan

_____

_____

_____

_____

_____

_____

_____

_____

_____

_____

_____

_____

_____

_____

_____

_____

_____

Dear Reader,

Now that you're done with this book, it is my hope that you take time to incorporate these rules into your life.

Rules without execution are dreams.

Take just one and incorporate it into your life every single day - for 30 days - and then let me know how you do. Don't be afraid to ask for help! Every great coach or athlete has assistance by way of a coach. Everyone who has achieved greatness in their lives has not done it alone.

Anybody can do anything for 30 days.
This thirty day challenge is designed to form a habit and make real change in your life. Everyone has an opinion about what you should do, but until you yourself commit to doing it, real and lasting change can't occur. Once you've nailed one rule, add another one and tackle it. If you'd like to invite others to join you on their own journey for accountability, that's great.

#StayOntheBall!

Steve